P9-DGD-458

BETTER TOGETHER

CONNECTING With GOD & OTHERS

Loveland, Colorado

Group

Group resources really work!

This Group resource incorporates our R.E.A.L. approach to ministry. It reinforces a growing friendship with Jesus, encourages long-term learning, and results in life transformation, because it's:

Relational—Learner-to-learner interaction enhances learning and builds Christian friendships.

Experiential—What learners experience through discussion and action sticks with them up to 9 times longer than what they simply hear or read.

Applicable—The aim of Christian education is to equip learners to be both hearers and doers of God's Word.

Learner-based—Learners understand and retain more when the learning process takes into consideration how they learn best.

Better Together: Connecting With God and Others

Copyright © 2013 Group Publishing, Inc.

Visit our website for more small group and church leadership resources: group.com

All rights reserved. No part of this book may be reproduced in any manner whatsoever without prior written permission from the publisher, except where noted in the text and in the case of brief quotations embodied in critical articles and reviews. For information, go to group.com/permissions.

Contributing Authors: Jeremy Amick, Bob D'Ambrosio, Eugenia Freiburger

Unless otherwise indicated, all Scripture quotations are taken from the *Holy Bible*, New Living Translation, copyright © 1996, 2004, 2007 by Tyndale House Foundation. Used by permission of Tyndale House Publishers, Inc., Carol Stream, Illinois 60188. All rights reserved.

ISBN 978-1-4707-0161-1
10 9 8 7 6 5 4 3 2   22 21 20 19 18 17 16 15 14 13
Printed in the United States of America.

Contents

Welcome!

Welcome to Group's E4:12 Bible Study Series. This series is focused on what God tells leaders in Ephesians 4:12—help people develop a greater understanding of how they are uniquely created and called to serve.

Whether you're new to the church or have been a part of it your whole life, you'll discover that we're all in this together. The heart of God's church is you! As you dig into the Bible passages for each session and reflect on the meaning for your life, you'll discover how God connects people to him through his church and through each other.

Each session concludes with an opportunity to discover how to put into practice what you've just learned—whether it's making changes in your own life, reaching out to others, or taking part in something bigger with your whole group involved. You'll have the chance to learn from the Bible and each other as you cultivate a better understanding of the plans God has for your life.

You are the church. We are the church. When we connect with other Jesus-followers—we're better together!

So again, welcome. We hope you'll find the experiences and studies here both meaningful and memorable.

Bob D'Am

—Bob D'Ambrosio, editor
bdambrosio@group.com

About the Sessions

Getting Started

Each session gives you tips and suggestions to ensure a great experience. You'll receive a list of items that may be needed for the session, along with ideas on how to maximize the experience. Read through this section first to make sure you're ready to go.

 ## Connecting With Others
(about 10 minutes)

This section connects group members with each other through a warm-up, mixer, or opportunity to get better acquainted. It's designed to be fun and informative and sets the tone for the rest of the study.

 ## Connecting With God
(about 35 minutes)

This is the central part of the session. The group will have the chance to interact with the Scripture passage. Through discussion and other sensory experiences, you'll learn how God's Word is relevant to *your* life.

 ## Connecting With Self
(about 10 minutes)

Now you'll move from understanding *how* the passage applies to your life, to thinking about ways you can *apply* it. In this part of the session, personal meaning is brought home through meaningful reflection and experiences.

Connecting With Prayer
(about 5 minutes)

One way we connect with God is through prayer. Each session will allow time for the group to experience personal prayer time using a variety of prayer formats.

Equipped 2 Serve

This is the "action step" part of the session. Each group member will reflect on how they will live out the session's main message in the weeks ahead. God equips us to serve others. Use the Equipped 2 Serve pages in this book as a journal to write down action plans, reflections, and God-sightings.

Facilitating This Study

The **bolded sections of text** in each session are for someone to read aloud to the group. This person could be the designated leader, or everyone could take turns so each person gets a chance to facilitate.

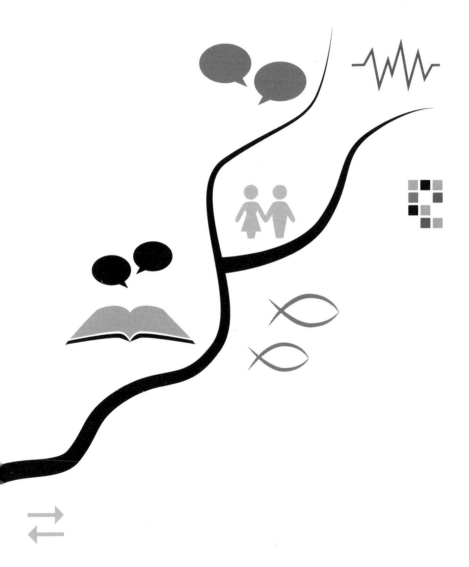

SESSION 1
We're Part of Something Bigger

The Point: The church is built on the faith of people.

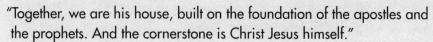

> **Key Verse:** Ephesians 2:20
>
> "Together, we are his house, built on the foundation of the apostles and the prophets. And the cornerstone is Christ Jesus himself."

Getting Started

Have each person in the group make a name tag as they arrive. Make sure chairs are arranged in a circle so everyone can connect visually. Got munchies? You may want to provide snacks or start a schedule for everyone to take turns providing a dessert.

Place a table near the seating area for group members, and lay a pillowcase in the center of the table. Pile small stones/river rocks on the pillowcase so there's enough for one per person.

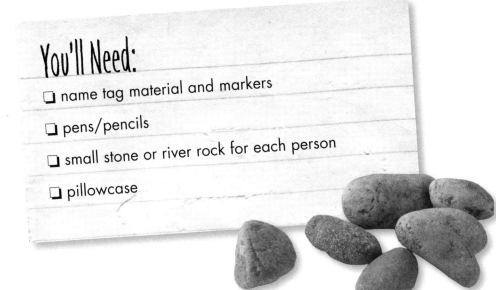

You'll Need:

- ☐ name tag material and markers
- ☐ pens/pencils
- ☐ small stone or river rock for each person
- ☐ pillowcase

Connecting With Others
(about 10 minutes)

Do you remember the nursery rhyme about the church from when you were a kid? You would fold your hands with your fingers on the inside, lift up your two index fingers, and say, "Here is the church, here is the steeple, open the doors, and see all the people." Let's try it! When you say "see all the people," open up your hands, but keep your fingers entwined. Now wiggle your fingers!

Pass your books around the room, and have each person write his or her name, phone number, and email address in the space provided on page 65. You can do this either at the beginning or end of your time together this session.

This simple illustration is not too far off from what God tells us about the church in the Bible. This Bible study will help us explore how God wants to connect with each of us and how he also desires for us to connect with each other. In this session, we'll explore how each of us is part of God's plan to build a strong church.

Get in groups of four and discuss:

Q If you could build your dream house, what would it look like?

Q What in your life is a foundation that keeps you steady during times of uncertainty?

Connecting With God
(about 35 minutes)

Have each person in the group select a small rock from the selection pile.

Have you ever wondered how the church came into existence? Is today's church what God had in mind? What exactly is the church? Let's see if we can answer these questions with an experiment.

Take a careful look at your rock. Feel it. Taste it if you want. What qualities do you find in your rock? Write these qualities in the box to the right. When everyone is finished writing, we'll share our observations.

Rock Qualities:

_____
_____
_____
_____
_____
_____
_____
_____

Which of these rock qualities are also desirable for a person? For a church?

Jesus recognized some of these qualities in Simon, one of his followers, when he asked his disciples a question. Read the section below from Matthew 16:13-18, and circle the word *rock* whenever it appears.

Matthew 16:13-18

"When Jesus came to the region of Caesarea Philippi, he asked his disciples, 'Who do people say that the Son of Man is?'

'Well,' they replied, 'some say John the Baptist, some say Elijah, and others say Jeremiah or one of the other prophets.'

Then he asked them, 'But who do you say I am?'

Simon Peter answered, 'You are the Messiah, the Son of the living God.'

Jesus replied, 'You are blessed, Simon son of John, because my Father in heaven has revealed this to you. You did not learn this from any human being. Now I say to you that you are Peter (which means 'rock'), and upon this rock I will build my church, and all the powers of hell will not conquer it.'"

Jesus recognized Simon's strong faith and tells him that he has been blessed personally, because God revealed his true identity to him. Jesus then gives him the special name of Peter ("petros" in Greek, referring to rock) to represent his rock-solid faith. It is this faith that ignited the beginning of the church. Jesus points ahead to the time when his disciples, his family of faith, will be called "my church." Jesus will build his church on the foundational faith of people who claim him as the "Messiah, the Son of the living God."

Why do you think Jesus wanted to know from his disciples what others believed about him?

Jesus flips the question from what others think about him to what the disciples think about him. What does this say to us regarding having knowledge about something versus having faith in something?

What did Jesus expect from Peter?

What do you think Jesus is expecting from his followers today?

Ephesians 2:20 gives us a better understanding of how God built his church.

Ephesians 2:20

"Together, we are his house, built on the foundation of the apostles and the prophets. And the cornerstone is Christ Jesus himself."

A cornerstone is the block that sets the form and function of a building. It's the stone builders lay first to make sure the alignment is correct. Jesus is the cornerstone of the church. He establishes a foundation through the faith of his followers who believe in him.

In what ways does the church today show evidence that Jesus is the cornerstone?

In what areas of your life is it evident that Jesus is the cornerstone?

 ## Connecting With Self
(about 10 minutes)

Ephesians 2:20 reminds us that *together* we make up God's church—his house. When Jesus-followers come together, they build a church that "the powers of hell" will not be able to destroy.

How can this Bible study group help you stay better connected to God and help you with your own personal faith development?

Think of an area in your life right now where you need Jesus to be the cornerstone for strength, guidance, and direction. Using a marker, write down one word or symbol on your rock that describes this area of your life. When you're done, place your rock on top of the pillowcase that's on our table.

Connecting With Prayer
(about 5 minutes)

God's church is people. The people who have faith in Jesus. We are God's church. Our rock pile symbolizes each of us coming together, forming God's church. As we build on the strength of each other, we build a stronger church. The pillowcase represents Jesus, the cornerstone. He is the foundation of the church.

Have each person grab a side of the pillowcase, and lift the pillowcase together to raise the pile of rocks.

Jesus lifts us up and brings us together to be his church. Let's spend a moment in silent prayer for the areas in our lives where we need Jesus to be the foundation.

After silent prayer time, have someone in the group pray:

Dear God, thank you for being the firm foundation that centers our lives. Thank you for bringing people of faith together to be your church. Help us to be strengthened daily through you and a support to strengthen each other. Amen.

Next time...

Date:_____ Time:_____

Place:_____

Equipped 2 Serve

Put your rock in your pocket and carry it around with you this week. Each time you feel it, let it be a reminder to pray for the area in your life where you need Jesus' help. Use this space to journal any discoveries or insights from this experience.

"For Jesus is the one referred to in the Scriptures, where it says, 'The stone that you builders rejected has now become the cornerstone.'" —Acts 4:11

SESSION 2
One Part Equals Many

The Point: Every Christian is part of the body of Christ.

> **Key Verse:** 1 Corinthians 12:27
>
> "All of you together are Christ's body, and each of you is a part of it."

Getting Started

If there are new group members this week, have each person make a name tag as they arrive. Be sure chairs are arranged in a circle so everyone can have eye contact. Make sure everyone feels welcome and at home.

You'll Need:

☐ name tag material and markers (as needed)

☐ pens/pencils

☐ large sheet of paper or whiteboard/flip chart, if available

Connecting With Others
(about 10 minutes)

Do you remember the cartoon series *The Jetsons?* Seems they had a robot for every task that needed to be done around the house. I wonder what the church would look like if it operated that way. Let's examine this concept a little closer.

In pairs, work together to develop a "ministry robot." Your robot will be limited to three functions that you feel are most important to the work of the church. The functions need to be very specific ministry tasks (not multi-tasks). For example, one task may include changing diapers in the nursery. You have 1 minute to determine three important ministry tasks your robot can do. List them in the box below.

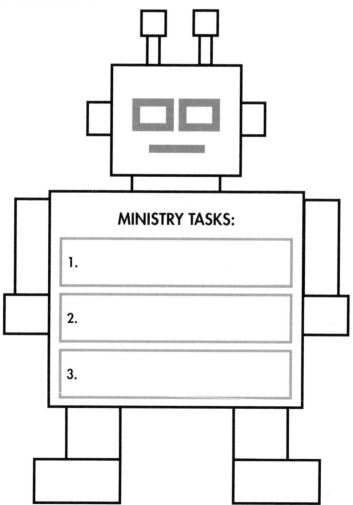

MINISTRY TASKS:

1.

2.

3.

Each pair should share the three ministry tasks their robot can accomplish with the rest of the group. Select someone to record these tasks on a sheet of paper (or whiteboard/flipchart, if available). Review the list to see the number of tasks included.

💬 **What would a local church look like if ministry tasks were *only* completed by *one* robot?**

💬 **How would it look different if the church had 10 ministry robots that completed 30 unique ministry tasks? 100 ministry robots?**

The church is not made up of robots. We're not robots. Yet, we are created by God with a ministry design. God has made us with a plan for our lives that coordinates perfectly with God's plan for the church.

Connecting With God
(about 35 minutes)

Each person in the church is essential. If each person were to fulfill a specific ministry task, God would be glorified and his church would be a powerful force for good. Consider these two definitions:

Synergy—The effective work of many parts functioning as a complete whole.

Individual Greatness—One part is superior in ability to the others and works independent of the whole.

Q Which of these strategies would be most effective for a sports team? A church ministry team?

Q When have you experienced a time when the synergy of a group created a powerful and positive outcome?

Let's examine a Scripture that speaks directly to the concept of how God designed each of us to fit into the synergy of his church.

Romans 12:4-5

"Just as our bodies have many parts and each part has a special function, so it is with Christ's body. We are many parts of one body, and we all belong to each other."

As we examine these verses, three concepts emerge that help us understand God's design for his church.

1. The church is *Christ's body*:

Paul makes a solid point here when he compares the church to the human body. We get that the brain does a different function than the heart. But he also explains something that may be more difficult to understand. The church is not ours. The body belongs to Christ.

How do you feel knowing you're part of the greater synergy of Christ's body? What are the advantages of being connected to something greater than you individually?

What does this Scripture say to someone who feels he or she is not an important part of the church?

2. The church is *one body*:

A second emphasis of this Scripture is that many people equal one. Christ's body, the church, is universal. The church is not segmented groups of people who work independent of each other in accomplishing God's goals. *All Christians are a part of Christ's body.* Together in Christ, we make a powerful and effective team.

With a partner, come up with a definition for the *church*. Write it in the box below, and share your definition when everyone is finished.

The church is..._____

_____

_____

_____

Let's keep these definitions of the church in mind as we examine the third point for the Romans 12 passage.

3. We belong to *one another*:

In these verses, Paul speaks to us concerning the concept of sharing.

Why is it critical that God's people share their gifts, abilities, money, time, and other resources?

Which of these resources do people find easiest to share? In what areas are people most reluctant?

God has given each of us gifts and talents to be shared. What we have belongs to the body. This includes all of our resources.

Every Christian is part of the body of Christ because God has created one team, the church. It is through his people that God accomplishes his work. Therefore, we have unity, even though we are all different in our abilities and experiences.

Connecting With Self
(about 10 minutes)

Invite group members to read the following verse and answer the questions below.

---

1 Corinthians 12:27

"All of you together are Christ's body, and each of you is a part of it."

💬 How do you see yourself being connected to your church?

💬 If you don't feel connected, what can you do to make that happen? How can this group help?

After everyone has had time to reflect on the questions, ask group members to share their insights.

Connecting With Prayer
(about 5 minutes)

Every Christian is part of the body of Christ. In 1 Thessalonians 5:11, we are given the command to "encourage each other and build each other up, just as you are already doing." Encouragement of others begins with prayer.

Let's go around our circle and affirm each other with prayerful encouragement. Spend a moment encouraging the person on your right, using this format:

Dear God, I thank you for (Name)**. Encourage** (Name) **in the area of** _____ .

Next time...

Date:_____ Time:_____

Place:_____

Equipped 2 Serve

The ministry of the church is a team effort. During this week, spend some time each day evaluating your role on this team. How has God equipped you for ministry? What are some burdens or needs in the local community that God has revealed to you? Pray that God would give you direction.

"It takes ten hands to make a basket."
—John Wooden, Basketball Hall of Fame Player and Coach

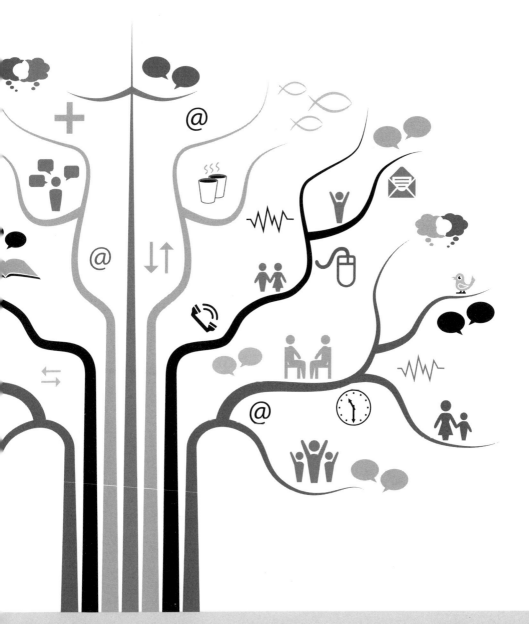

SESSION 3
Wonderfully Made

The Point: God uniquely creates all people for special service.

Key Verse: Romans 12:6

"In his grace, God has given us different gifts for doing certain things well."

Getting Started

Enjoy getting to know group members as everyone arrives. Continue using name tags if there are new people to the group. Consider providing "fun size" candy bars for group members to enjoy as they arrive and mingle.

You'll Need:

- ❏ name tag material and markers (as needed)
- ❏ pens/pencils
- ❏ "fun size" candy bars (optional)
- ❏ hammer or any other kind of workman's tool (optional)

Connecting With Others
(about 10 minutes)

If available, enjoy some candy as we connect with each other.

Welcome! In this session, we'll be looking at the reason why God created us all so uniquely different. Like candy, we each have our own flavor.

💬 **What is your favorite candy? Why?**

We're going to pretend for a moment that we work in a candy factory. You are going to create a new candy bar that will be marketed worldwide. You must use at least two ingredients for the interior of the bar and at least one for the outside of the bar. For example, a Snickers bar has peanuts, caramel, and nougat on the inside and is coated with milk chocolate on the outside.

Using the design below, create your own candy bar by listing your secret ingredients.

My Special Bar

Exterior Ingredients:

Interior Ingredients:

Have each person share the ingredients of their special bar, and then discuss:

Which of the newly created candy bars in our group appeals to you the most? Why?

Why are there so many candy bars available today?

Like candy, when we look at God's creation, we see a magnificent variety of all things—different plants, intriguing animals, and awesome landscapes. And when we look at God's crowning creation—us—we discover that *each person* has been uniquely and wonderfully made.

Connecting With God
(about 35 minutes)

Let's read aloud Psalm 139:14 together.

Psalm 139:14

"Thank you for making me so wonderfully complex! Your workmanship is marvelous—how well I know it."

Notice the point that the psalmist makes about the God who knows all things—it is our Creator who determines our unique characteristics.

Let's experience our uniqueness with a simple experiment using the paper person on the page to the right.

Think of something you recently accomplished that you're proud of. Or, think of something you do well or an activity you enjoy. Write this down on the paper person in the area that would represent the action. For example, you may write "sang in the choir for the Christmas program" on the paper person's mouth.

Share what you wrote down on your paper person with the group. As others share, write *their* name in the location they identified on *your* paper person.

Take a look at your paper person. What does it tell you about the gifts and talents represented in this group?

What would be the outcome if everyone in the church had the same interest or talent and used it in the same way?

💬 **What does this tell us about why God created us differently?**

There's a plan as to why we're each different and unique. In Romans 12, Paul makes the connection between who we *are* and what we *do*.

Romans 12:4-8

"Just as our bodies have many parts and each part has a special function, so it is with Christ's body. We are many parts of one body, and we all belong to each other. In his grace, God has given us different gifts for doing certain things well. So if God has given you the ability to prophesy, speak out with as much faith as God has given you. If your gift is serving others, serve them well. If you are a teacher, teach well. If your gift is to encourage others, be encouraging. If it is giving, give generously. If God has given you leadership ability, take the responsibility seriously. And if you have a gift for showing kindness to others, do it gladly."

Let's examine this passage for a few minutes. There are three truths to discover that describe God's purpose for creating us differently.

Truth #1: Each part has a special function.

When Paul mentions that we each have a special function in the body of Christ, it's like looking into a large toolbox. A toolbox usually includes a variety of tools that are used for specific purposes. Let's take a hammer for example. Hold up a hammer, if available.

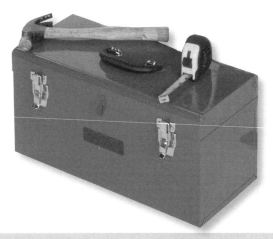

How is this tool designed to accomplish a specific purpose?

What is the danger of using this tool in a way that is unintended?

God has given the church tools for ministry. These tools are the gifts and abilities that are unique to each member of the body.

Truth #2: God has given us different gifts for doing certain things well.

God has a purpose for giving each Christian a different gift for ministry. When we use these gifts in the way God has called us, then our effort is effective. On the other hand, if we neglect or misuse our gifts, the body of Christ is not as functional. Let's think again about the use of a hammer.

There are ways you could use a hammer other than to drive a nail into wood. For example, instead of using a screwdriver to insert a screw into your living room wall, you could use a hammer. However, the outcome could be messy. We are created by God with "tools" that increase our effectiveness in ministry.

Which one of your gifts (tools) makes you feel the most effective and the most useful?

Truth #3: We must use what we have been given.

As Paul explains in this passage, we must not neglect our gifts for ministry. Let's think about tools one more time.

Imagine this scene: You see someone attempting to drive a large nail into wood using his or her bare hands. Then you notice the person has a hammer within 3 feet of his or her reach.

When have you felt like you were doing a task without having the right tools?

Knowing what tools you've been given helps you discover the tasks you're equipped to do.

Connecting With Self
(about 10 minutes)

For a few moments, let's reflect on what may be in our own "ministry toolbox." Silently answer the questions below. After you've had time to think through these questions, find a partner and share any discoveries.

What was the most enjoyable task, experience, or ministry project that you've been involved with during the last year?

What was the result of your involvement?

Based on that experience, what gifts or abilities do you feel God has provided for you to be successful?

Connecting With Prayer
(about 5 minutes)

Sports teams often huddle together before, during, and after a game to encourage one another on the team. Let's stand and form a huddle. Place your right arm in the center, and pile your hand on top of the others. Let's go around the circle and pray for the person to our right using this format:

God, we praise you for (name of the person to the right) **because** _____.

Next time...

Date:_____ Time:_____

Place:_____

Equipped 2 Serve

Consider three people who are closest to you. Using email, a phone call, or in-person conversation, ask these three people to assess the following:

💬 What is one skill or ability that you see as my greatest strength?

💬 What is one example of a time you have seen me use this skill or ability effectively?

Spend a few moments this week in prayer, asking God to use the responses from others as a guide for what he's equipped you to do. Ask God how he can use your gifts and abilities to strengthen your church and community.

"Let your good deeds shine out for all to see, so that everyone will praise your heavenly Father." —Matthew 5:16

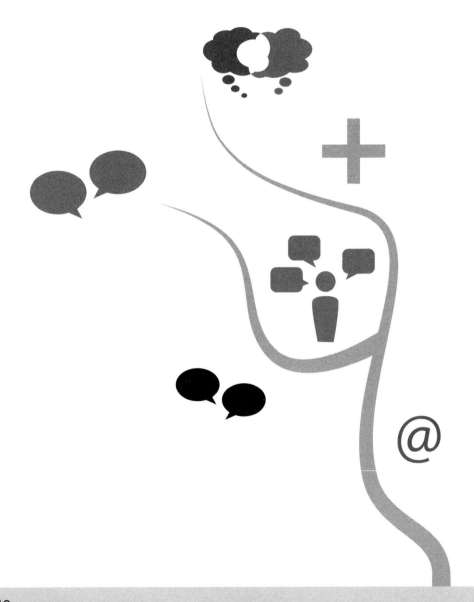

SESSION 4

Playing My Part

The Point: God's invitation to serve is given to every Christian.

> **Key Verse:** 1 Peter 2:9
>
> "But you are not like that, for you are a chosen people. You are royal priests, a holy nation, God's very own possession. As a result, you can show others the goodness of God, for he called you out of the darkness into his wonderful light."

Getting Started

Arrange chairs so everyone can sit together in a circle. Provide name tags if people are still unfamiliar with everyone's names.

Find a CD of orchestra (instrumental only) music or get access to a radio station before the session starts. Many smart phones can access Internet radio such as Pandora or AccuRadio. You can also check your local library's media department for a classical music CD.

You'll Need:

- ❏ name tag material and markers (as needed)
- ❏ pens/pencils
- ❏ CD or radio station of instrumental music
- ❏ CD player (as needed)

Connecting With Others
(about 10 minutes)

During this study, we've been examining how we can connect with God and each other. In this session, we'll discover how each Christ-follower is a part of God's plan for the church. Let's get started.

To help us focus, close your eyes and listen to this music.

Play 1 minute of classical orchestra music from the radio or a CD. In groups of four, discuss:

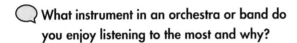 **What instrument in an orchestra or band do you enjoy listening to the most and why?**

Enjoy getting to know each other as you're waiting for everyone to arrive. Be friendly and introduce yourself to others you haven't met. Try to learn one new thing about someone in the group before the session begins.

How is the church like or unlike an orchestra?

The church can be compared to an orchestra or band. Like a group of musicians, the people in a church work together to make a sound that's unique and harmonious. Today we'll focus on how God asks us to "play our instrument" or do our part in serving. We need to understand this concept in order to see God's plan for each of us. We're all part of it. We're all in this together.

Connecting With God
(about 35 minutes)

Have you ever counted how many roles or titles you fulfill? In the box to the right, make a list of each of those roles, such as father, son, manager, etc.

Did anyone write down that they are a "priest"? How about being "chosen by God"? Actually, both these titles could go on everyone's list. Let's read more about this concept in 1 Peter 2:9.

My Roles:

---

1 Peter 2:9

"But you are a chosen people, a royal priesthood, a holy nation, God's special possession, that you may declare the praises of him who called you out of darkness into his wonderful light." (NIV)

In the Old Testament, the "priesthood" system was the way people connected to God for spiritual care, forgiveness of sins, and representation on their behalf. In the New Testament, Jesus now fulfills this priestly system. We no longer have to go to an earthly priest to connect with God. The door to God's presence, once manned by Old Testament priests, is now open to all. Jesus explains this concept by telling his followers that because God calls us his "chosen people" and a "royal priesthood," we are now given the privilege to carry out the "priestly" functions of serving and caring for others.

Which of these terms (chosen people, royal priesthood, holy nation, special possession) surprises you the most and why?

The primary role of the Old Testament priest was to serve God and, as a result, serve people. God calls us to the team to serve his people. Serve his church. Be the church.

💬 Who has been a "priest" to you in some way—without being an official member of the clergy?

💬 When have you had the opportunity to come alongside someone and be a "priest"?

Paul has some advice on this in Romans 12:6-8.

Romans 12:6-8

"We have different gifts, according to the grace given to each of us. If your gift is prophesying, then prophesy in accordance with your faith; if it is serving, then serve; if it is teaching, then teach; if it is to encourage, then give encouragement; if it is giving, then give generously; if it is to lead, do it diligently; if it is to show mercy, do it cheerfully." (NIV)

Circle the words *if* and *then* in this Scripture. Paul presents a pattern in these verses. If.....then. *If* you have been given a gift or ability—*then* use it. In a later session, we'll explore the gifts we've been given, but for now, let's focus on the call to action.

💬 Why do you think Paul keeps making the same point, using different gifts as examples?

💬 How is Paul's teaching similar to the Nike slogan "Just Do It"?

 **Connecting With Self**
(about 10 minutes)

God calls us to be a part of his "holy nation." He wants us to be part of the orchestra so that together we can make music that will minister to those around us.

Complete this sentence:
If I have been given the ability to _____
then I will_____.

In what area of your life right now might you need a new direction if you're going to be a part of God's "priesthood"? How willing are you to let God set the course for that new direction?

Connecting With Prayer
(about 5 minutes)

Turn to page 48, and write a prayer inside the cross about the sentence you completed in the "Connecting With Self" section. Your prayer could ask God to help you move forward in making this happen, confess to a barrier that keeps you from serving, or express desire to be more aware of opportunities around you. After you've written your prayer, hold the cross to your heart, offering the prayer silently and personally to God.

Have someone in the group play a selection of the orchestra music for reflection during the prayer time. After a time of silent prayer, have someone in the group pray:

Dear God, thank you for calling us to be part of your holy nation. Thank you for calling us to the priesthood of believers. Lead us in ways that we can serve others according to the abilities you've given us. Help us to see the needs around us and how we can help those in need. Amen.

Next time...

Date:_____ Time:_____

Place:_____

Equipped 2 Serve

This week focuses on opportunities God presents for you to be a "priest" to someone in need. Allow God to work through you in precisely the way he designed you to function. Make notes below of any opportunities that present themselves this week and how you responded. Pray for God to lead you and for the strength to make a difference in someone's life this week.

"Life's most persistent and urgent question is: What are you doing for others?" —Martin Luther King, Jr.

SESSION 5

Ready, Set, Action

The Point: Who we are defines our purpose.

Key Verse: Ephesians 4:11-13

"Now these are the gifts Christ gave to the church: the apostles, the prophets, the evangelists, and the pastors and teachers. Their responsibility is to equip God's people to do his work and build up the church, the body of Christ. This will continue until we all come to such unity in our faith and knowledge of God's Son that we will be mature in the Lord, measuring up to the full and complete standard of Christ."

Getting Started

Be sure seating is arranged in a circle to create a feeling of community. Any new members? If so, make sure everyone is introduced. Got snacks? Sometimes sharing a treat helps people feel more welcome.

Gather an assortment of kitchen utensils (forks, knives, spoons, tongs, ladles, etc.) and make sure there is at least one utensil for every two people in your group. Place in a central location for use in the "Connecting With Self" section.

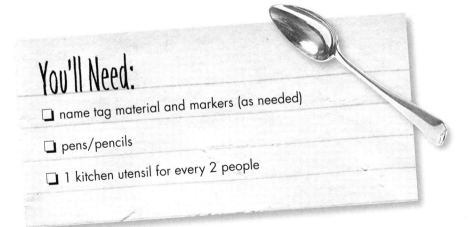

You'll Need:

- ☐ name tag material and markers (as needed)
- ☐ pens/pencils
- ☐ 1 kitchen utensil for every 2 people

Connecting With Others
(about 10 minutes)

During this study, we've been examining how to connect with God and each other. In this session, we'll discover that *who we are* defines our purpose. We'll understand that we are created to be part of God's church and to serve in God's church. Let's get started.

Everyone connects with God differently. We tend to perceive and experience God best through our individual styles.

Close your eyes and think of a song about God that's your favorite. You can also think of any inspirational song that comes to mind, as long as it makes you think of who God is or what help he provides for your life. Everyone have a song in mind?

💬 Share your song title with the group. What does your song say about God? Why is this song one of your favorites?

💬 What qualities of God are mentioned in these songs?

Did you hear all the attributes of God we just listed? We each experience God in our own unique way. In the Bible, King David acknowledged that we are fearfully and wonderfully made (Psalm 139:14). We are unique individuals created in the image of God, meaning that we have a God-given capacity to experience God. That means we perceive and experience God through who we are. Who we are affects how we perceive God. Who we are also helps to define our God-given purpose(s). Let's examine this concept further.

Connecting With God
(about 35 minutes)

Paul speaks to some of the roles and functions that God gives the church. Let's read what he has to say about this in Ephesians.

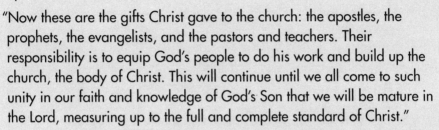

Ephesians 4:11-13

"Now these are the gifts Christ gave to the church: the apostles, the prophets, the evangelists, and the pastors and teachers. Their responsibility is to equip God's people to do his work and build up the church, the body of Christ. This will continue until we all come to such unity in our faith and knowledge of God's Son that we will be mature in the Lord, measuring up to the full and complete standard of Christ."

Paul writes this letter to the church in Ephesus at a time when they were struggling with false teachings, internal bickering, and the pull of their secular culture. He cheers them on to overcome these obstacles and work together to build up the church. Paul mentions that those in leadership roles, such as apostles, prophets, evangelists, pastors, and teachers, are to do one thing: equip God's people to build up the church.

◯ What is involved in the process of equipping someone?

◯ How have you been equipped to build up the church?

◯ Where in your life are you in a role to equip someone else? How are you making sure that happens?

Paul was encouraging all who followed Jesus to maintain their commitment, grow in their spiritual maturity, and keep unity in the body. And today God still provides his church with the needed gifts, talents, and roles to build the church up and contribute to the church's unity! Each of us is both a gift *to* God's church AND gifted *for* God's church.

How does working together as a group—the church—create the "full and complete standard" of Christ? Why may this not be possible alone?

The overarching reason God gives apostles, prophets, and teachers to his church is to prepare God's people for works of service, to build up the church, and experience the fullness of Christ. Each role has a purpose that is specific to the collaborative process of equipping God's people. Said another way, who we are defines our purposes.

What gifts do you feel God has given you to support the work of the church? How are you currently using those gifts to build up the church?

Connecting With Self
(about 10 minutes)

We started our session reflecting on how we perceive and experience God through who we are. Who we are helps define our God-given purpose. We've learned that we are all called to unity in Christ, to grow in maturity in Christ, and reflect the full and complete picture of Jesus. Let's experience how this actually works.

Have everyone find a partner and together select one kitchen utensil from the pile.

In pairs, determine a different function that your utensil may accomplish. For example, a fork could be a backscratcher.

When every pair has determined a unique function for their utensil, have everyone share their ideas.

Which use of your utensil is the most effective? How is this like or unlike when people serve in a role that matches their gifting?

How would you define your "sweet spot" or primary area where you can be most effective in serving?

Just as the function of these utensils defines their role, God equips us with abilities that help shape and define our purpose.

Connecting With Prayer
(about 5 minutes)

Let's focus on the ideas we've learned from this session with a time of reflective prayer. Please stand, form a circle, and follow the prompts as we spend time in quiet reflection. Lead participants in the actions indicated within the parentheses throughout the prayer.

Dear God, we stand before you recognizing you as the creator of all things. *(Hold out your hands with your palms up.)* [Pause]

Thank you for making us special and unique with many gifts, talents, and skills. [Pause] *(Now close your hands to make a fist.)*

Forgive us for the times we've been closed to opportunities to serve you. Utilize our abilities for the benefit of others and your church. [Pause] *(Now place your hands on your heart.)*

Fill our hearts with the fullness of knowing your Son and becoming mature in our faith. [Pause] *(Now join hands with those around you.)*

May your church be built up through each of us...and in unity of our love for you. [Pause] **Amen.**

Next time...

Date:_____ Time:_____

Place:_____

Equipped 2 Serve

As you go through the week, focus on the fact that you are both a gift *to* God's church and gifted *for* God's church.

Write down the various gifts, talents, and abilities God has given you. Next to each, write how you can use those functions to help those near you grow closer to Christ.

"Strange, isn't it? Each man's life touches so many other lives. When he isn't around he leaves an awful hole, doesn't he?"
—Clarence the Angel, *It's a Wonderful Life*

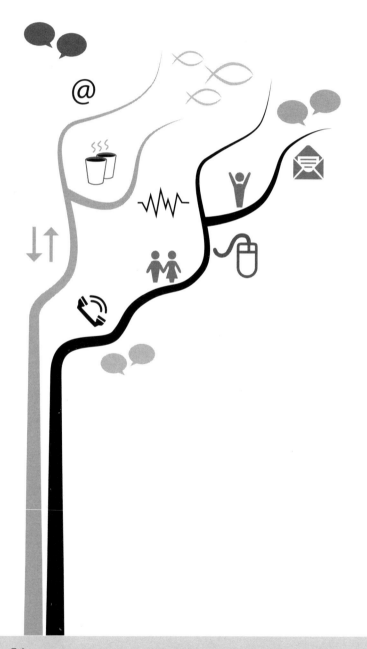

SESSION 6
Connected to Grow

The Point: We bear fruit by connecting with Jesus.

> **Key Verse:** John 15:7-9
>
> "But if you remain in me and my words remain in you, you may ask for anything you want, and it will be granted! When you produce much fruit, you are my true disciples. This brings great glory to my Father. I have loved you even as the Father has loved me. Remain in my love."

Getting Started

Since this is the last session, consider some celebration snacks, a special meal, or a yummy dessert! Be sure to arrange seating in a circle so everyone feels connected. Acknowledge anyone that's new and make sure everyone has an opportunity to introduce themselves.

Purchase a small grapevine wreath from a craft store. Cut the wreath into 6-inch segments so you have a piece of vine for each person. If a wreath is not available, consider using sections of a small tree branch, rope, twine, or piece of string. You'll use these 6-inch pieces for the closing prayer experience.

You'll Need:

☐ name tag material and markers (as needed)

☐ pens/pencils

☐ 6-inch piece of vine for each person

Connecting With Others

(about 10 minutes)

This is the last chapter of our study. In this session, we'll focus on the fact that we're better together when we're connected with God and each other. Let's get started.

Can you think of a time in your life when you really needed someone—a helper, encourager, supporter, coach, or friend? In pairs, share a time when having a helper/buddy made a difference in your life or situation.

Have group members come back together and share the role of the person who made a difference in their life (friend, spouse, teacher, etc.).

Look at all the different ways God has placed people in our lives. We were created to be in relationships. We need God and we need each other. We are better together when we experience community. Perhaps the Bible verse that makes this point most clearly is Ecclesiastes 4:9-10. Let's read this together.

Ecclesiastes 4:9-10

"Two people are better off than one, for they can help each other succeed. If one person falls, the other can reach out and help. But someone who falls alone is in real trouble."

Connecting With God
(about 35 minutes)

The wise author in Ecclesiastes was writing to a people in need of meaning and identity. The Hebrew people were in captivity in Babylon and needed words of wisdom about how life can be best lived. The writer states that two are better than one and the person who has no one is to be pitied. God created us to live in community and to need one another—to need a friend, helper, buddy. Life is designed for companionship, not isolation.

Who in your life right now is helping you succeed?

How does this principle (two are better than one) make the church stronger?

We not only need each other but, more importantly, we need Jesus. In the Gospel of John, we see a glimpse of one of the most important thoughts and teachings of Jesus. Let's read John 15:7-9.

John 15:7-9

"But if you remain in me and my words remain in you, you may ask for anything you want, and it will be granted! When you produce much fruit, you are my true disciples. This brings great glory to my Father. I have loved you even as the Father has loved me. Remain in my love."

Jesus spent time talking about the importance of remaining connected to him, the vine. The disciples were very familiar with vineyards and understood the importance of the branches remaining attached to a very strong, hardy vine.

Healthy, connected branches are richly colored green, vibrantly growing, and ultimately produce fruit—grapes. Eventually, these grapes accomplish their ultimate place of service and purpose—providing nourishment. A branch not rightly connected to the vine is fruitless, lacks vibrant color, withers, and dries out.

💬 How are you connected to the "vine"? Which of these stages best describes your connection to Jesus and why?

❑ Producing fruit

❑ Growing vibrantly

❑ Withering as we speak

❑ Drying out dangerously

Jesus said, "If you remain in me…." Some translations use the word *abide* instead of *remain*. We don't use the word abide today in our everyday conversation. It's a verb that means to dwell or to linger. In other words, Jesus was saying if we make our home with him and if we dwell together with him, we will produce works of service—fruit. And the result? We bring great joy to God.

💬 How can you remain close to Jesus? What changes need to happen in your life right now in order to make that happen?

💬 Where in your life are you bearing fruit?

Jesus knew that abiding in him gives us strength, life, courage, and the ability to produce fruit. We are better together with Jesus!

Connecting With Self
(about 10 minutes)

Let's revisit the concept of producing fruit. Think of ways in which your "fruit" can bring great glory to God. How might these good works do good for others? In the grapes on page 64, write down two or three ways in which you can serve others with the fruit you're producing.

Have each person share with the group one of the actions they've identified.

How can our group support you in this effort?

Connecting With Prayer
(about 5 minutes)

Distribute the pieces of grapevine that have been prepared. Have all group members stand together in a circle. Ask the members to hold out their grapevine section and connect it end to end with the other pieces to form one continuous circle. When everyone is connected, have someone in the group pray:

Dear God, thank you for loving us so much that you sent Jesus to connect with each of us. Help us to abide in you so we may produce works that serve others. Remind us that there is strength in cooperation and that we don't have to go it alone. Amen.

Next time...

Date:_____ Time:_____

Place:_____

Equipped 2 Serve

As you go through the week, make notes of the actions you've taken to abide with God. Chart your progress and note any evidence of producing fruit as a result.

"The tree that grows by the river bank does not suffer the effect of drought." —African proverb

GETTING CONNECTED

Pass your books around the room, and have everyone write his or her name, phone number, and email address.

Name _____

Phone _____

Email _____

Name _____

Phone _____

Email _____

Name _____

Phone _____

Email _____

Name _____

Phone _____

Email _____

Name _____

Phone _____

Email _____

Name _____

Phone _____

Email _____

Name _____

Phone _____

Email _____

Name _____

Phone _____

Email _____

Name _____

Phone _____

Email _____

Name _____

Phone _____

Email _____

Name _____

Phone _____

Email _____

Name _____

Phone _____

Email _____

Name _____

Phone _____

Email _____

Name _____

Phone _____

Email _____

Name _____

Phone _____

Email _____

Name _____

Phone _____

Email _____

Name _____

Phone _____

Email _____

PRAYER REQUESTS

Request: _____

_____

_____

Name: _____ Date:_____

Request: _____

_____

_____

Name: _____ Date:_____

Request: _____

_____

_____

Name: _____ Date:_____

Request: _____

_____

_____

Name: _____ Date:_____

Request: _____

_____

_____

Name: _____ Date:_____

PRAYER REQUESTS

Request: _____

_____

_____

Name: _____ Date:_____

Request: _____

_____

_____

Name: _____ Date:_____

Request: _____

_____

_____

Name: _____ Date:_____

Request: _____

_____

_____

Name: _____ Date:_____

Request: _____

_____

_____

Name: _____ Date:_____

PRAYER REQUESTS

Request: _____

_____

_____

Name: _____ Date:_____

Request: _____

_____

_____

Name: _____ Date:_____

Request: _____

_____

_____

Name: _____ Date:_____

Request: _____

_____

_____

Name: _____ Date:_____

Request: _____

_____

_____

Name: _____ Date:_____

PRAYER REQUESTS

Request: _____

_____

_____

Name: _____ Date:_____

Request: _____

_____

_____

Name: _____ Date:_____

Request: _____

_____

_____

Name: _____ Date:_____

Request: _____

_____

_____

Name: _____ Date:_____

Request: _____

_____

_____

Name: _____ Date:_____

PRAYER REQUESTS

Request: _____

_____

_____

Name: _____ Date:_____

Request: _____

_____

_____

Name: _____ Date:_____

Request: _____

_____

_____

Name: _____ Date:_____

Request: _____

_____

_____

Name: _____ Date:_____

Request: _____

_____

_____

Name: _____ Date:_____